James Abraham Martling

London Bridge

Or, a capital and labor. A poem for the times

James Abraham Martling

London Bridge
Or, a capital and labor. *A poem for the times*

ISBN/EAN: 9783337006389

Printed in Europe, USA, Canada, Australia, Japan

Cover: Foto ©Thomas Meinert / pixelio.de

More available books at **www.hansebooks.com**

LONDON BRIDGE;

OR,

CAPITAL AND LABOR.

𝔄 𝔓𝔬𝔢𝔪 𝔣𝔬𝔯 𝔱𝔥𝔢 𝔗𝔦𝔪𝔢𝔰.

BY

PROFESSOR JAMES A. MARTLING.

For heaven holds men of one degree ;
An equal-born fraternity.

BOSTON:

JAMES H. EARLE, PUBLISHER,

20 HAWLEY STREET.

1881.

PREFATORY NOTE.

PROFESSOR MARTLING'S complete poetical works, in one volume, will soon be given to the public. "Los Angeles," which first appeared in the San Francisco Bulletin, and was copied by our western and New York papers, was by many public men called a "little gem." Rev. M. L. Williston, now in Germany, writes, "I pronounce it a modern classic."

Of his last poem, on "Death," Wendell Phillips says, "I think the Professor's verses very striking and beautiful, and the lines are exquisitely finished."

This forthcoming collection of Poems contains vivid pictures of every-day life. Some of them have become historic, dating back to anti-slavery times.

Professor Martling translated Homer's "Illiad," but had only published the first Book. The following are some of the criticisms sent him:

Hon. Wm. E. Gladstone, Prime Minister of England, said of it, "It seems to me to do him great credit."

Wendell Phillips wrote, "It shows great mastery of the original, and rare power of language."

Dr. Post of St. Louis : "The translation seems to me scholarly, and executed with rare fidelity and exactness of correspondence, in word and thought, to the original : at the same time it is poetic in diction, and with rhythmic harmony of structure."

"London Bridge " was written at Spadra, in 1878, but the "Prologue" and "Workingmen's Song" were writen in 1880.

Song of the Workingmen.

SONG OF THE WORKINGMEN.

WE be workingmen, we!
Ours be shoulders labor-worn,
Arms of brawn and hands of horn;
Still, though sometimes overborne, —
Still, though toil be paid with scorn, —
    Independent we!

Not of the commune, we!
Corn should grow for him who delves;
Heaven helps them that help themselves;
But the secret tens and twelves
Nurse a host of sponging elves!
    Not of the Jacobins, we!

11

Not of the anarchists, we !
In this country of the free,
All is hope for you and me ;
If there something higher be,
Who should have it, if not we ?
   Not of the levelers, we !

Not of agrarians, we !
Labor is not all a curse !
Toil is hard, but crime is worse !
Have we but an empty purse,
That the morrow may reverse !
   Not of the sand-lot, we !

Not of infidels, we !
Nay, and even if we were,
Could a fellow-laborer
To such Leader dare demur,

As the Christ — the Carpenter ?
 Nay, no infidels, we !

We are workingmen, we !
Christ His followers thus addressed ;
Whoso asks to be confessed
Chief of all and lordliest,
Should be servant to the rest !
 We are servants, we !

Though we journeymen be,
Sometimes tramps, unhoused, unfed,
Wanderers disinherited !
Still, of Some One was it said :
" Not a where to lay his head ! '
 " Tramps ? " — And what was He ?

We be laborers, we !

We behold benignant eyes,

Bending on us from the skies,

Telling us that we can rise,

Only through self-sacrifice !

We be workingmen, we !

PROLOGUE.

FAIREST of lands ! Sole home of liberty !

Land of the free ! — the equal home of all !

Land of my love ! I have a fear for thee

Lest the strong arches of thy fabric fall

Into remediless ruin, as the wall

Of haughty Nineveh ; and one shall sit —

Him hap, who on the ruins of St. Paul

Sits to sketch London Bridge — and add to it

Thee too, when *Troja fuit*, shall of thee be

     writ.

I fear for thee, lest of the pillared state,

Through lust of office, and the greed of gain,

Thine equal arches from unequal weight,

Topple and plunge into the depths amain.

2   17

The clamors of the poor — thy cry of pain
My mother in thine agony! — the stay —
The pier is groaning 'neath the unwonted
        strain,
And battlement and buttress may give away!
God in His infinite pity long avert the day!

Yet not the commune — not the levelers
Who always level downward — to the poor
Are their best friends.   The crude philoso-
        phers
From gorge and lapstone — ignorant and
        sure
Because so ignorant, — they can never cure
The ills of social order! — and, indeed,
The ill is not all ill, and to endure
Is manly, were it ill.   The better creed
Is this — 'tis Christ's — let each regard his
        brother's need.

All is not ill, if rightly understood ;
That is not ill that stirs the inner fire ;
The inequalities of life are good :
They serve to quicken us — to wake desire
For wealth it may be -- or for somewhat
      higher.
And the low hind, whom pinching want
      compels
To ceaseless labor, if his want inspire
Him to incessant struggle, he excels
Himself thereby, and may attain to some-
      thing else.   .

And charity and gentle sympathy —
The fellow-feeling for a brother's woe —
Are ever born of dire necessity !
Ah ! if there were no want, we must forego
The fountains sweet of tenderness, that glow

From the full heart of pity — bubbling o'er
In kindly deeds, that human nature show
Still Godlike in commiseration for
The Master's poor — that we have with us
    evermore!

The "Builder of the Bridge" — the "Ponti
    Fex!"
Termed wisely thus the ancient Roman race,
Their highest priest, who wielded both the
    Rex
That symbolized religion, and the mace
Of office in the commonwealth's chief place—
Head of the church and state at once.   If we
As wisely could conjoin the strength and
    grace
Of law and love, there could no danger be,
Land of my birth, I then should have no
    fear for thee!

LONDON BRIDGE.

SARAH and Bessie,
  And Lucy and Lily,
And Jack and Jessie,
And Tom and Tilly,
All were playing at London Bridge,
While at the door was Little Midge,
Holding her dolly to her breast,
Watching and dreaming about the rest.

23

Back and forth they swayed and swung,
And a childish ditty sung ;
O'er and o'er, again, again,
One monotonous refrain,
" *London Bridge is fallen down,*
Fallen down, fallen down,
London Bridge is fallen down,   •
My fair lady !"

II.

The wind was blowing up from the sea,
Lightly caressing forehead and hair,
Kissing them all, the brown and the fair ; —
For Heaven holds men of one degree,
An equal-born fraternity, —
And all were on a level there.
Plain their garb, but necklace and crown
Fell from the largess of the sun ;

Gem and jewel were raining down,

Flecking and decking every one, —

Decking them all, the brown and the fair,

For all were on a level there, —

For heaven holds men of one degree,

An equal-born fraternity!

Back and forth they swayed and swung!

O'er and o'er their song they sung;

One monotonous refrain,

Like the patter of the rain,

Like the moan of summer's breeze,

Like the hum of summer's bees, —

Like the wash of silver seas,

Over strands of silvern sands; —

Like a symphony of bells, —

Like the song of ocean shells, —

Like the noises of a town

    In a dreamy land!

" London Bridge is fallen down —
Fallen down — fallen down !
London Bridge is fallen down,

    My lady fair! "

Happy, happy childhood's days !
Happy, happy childhood's plays !
Healthful limbs and hearts of feather !
  Every joint and thew astrain, —
  Tugging with their might and main ! —
Pulsing, struggling together !
All the sport is in the strife !
Face to face and might to might,
So they keep the bridge aright !
Ah ! that thus it were with life !
Happy, happy childhood's years !
All were fellows there and peers !

III.

This was in the long ago ;
Some are wrinkled now, and old ;
Some are in the church-yard mold,
Sleeping where the roses grow !
" London Bridge is fallen down, fallen down,
Fallen down !
London Bridge is fallen down,
My lady fair ! "

This was in the long ago,
Little, — little do we know
What the future hath in store —
What there is that lieth before
Any of us, — if there be at our feet
Bridal robe, or winding sheet !

IV.

Ah, 't were better to be dead,
Than forsaking love and truth,
With disdain and scorn to tread
On the playmates of our youth!

It were better to be dead,
Than from truth and love to part,
And to live and have it said,
" His is dry-rot of the heart!"

It were better to be dead,
Than to live with heavy purse, —
Heavy with the price of bread, —
Heavy with the poor man's curse!

It were better to be dead,
Than with leprous soul and feet,
Drag, as felons, to the *Dread*
Presence of the judgment seat!

It were better to be dead, —
Better — better in the grave,
Than survive our manhood fled,
And to be a rich man's slave!

It were better to be dead,
Than to see our kith and kin —
E'en the wife whose youth we wed, —
Pale with want, and hunger thin!

It were better to be dead,
Than to live and curse our kind, —
Tramping with despairing tread,
For the work we cannot find!

It were better to be dead,
Than to hear the hopeless cry
Of our little ones for bread!
Christ! it were not hard to die!

VI.

London Bridge is fallen down !
Arch and buttress all are gone :
Truss and beam and massy stone,
All by time are overthrown ; —
And the fragments scattered far,
Like the fragments of a star ; —
Some perhaps with fire divine,
And self-luminous, to shine ;
In the empyrean to burn,
Symbols of the soul eterne ! —
Wanderers some, from place to place,
Planets, fugitive through space,
Through the boundless void of heaven,
Into utter darkness driven !

The Old London Bridge.

VII.

London Bridge is fallen down !

Arching way and battlement,

Wedded beams asunder rent,

In the floods to surge and drown ?

Jeweled sunbeams tripping o'er,

Tread the dimpled arms no more !

Flitting smiles, and love and pride,

Dash no more from side to side !

Laugh no more, nor boisterous shout,

From the angles leapeth out !

Here and there the fragments strown,

London Bridge is fallen down !

VIII.

Sarah long ago was wed

To a thrifty Yorkshire farmer,

And they called her Mrs. Armor :

And the simple life she led,

Made her healthful and content, —

Kept her sweet and innocent :

For the plenty of her board,

Blesses she the loving Lord ;

Grudging not nor crust nor sigh,

For the homeless passer-by,

But with tears her eyes bedim,

As she looketh upon him,

And she scarce can get her breath

As unto herself she saith :

" *London Bridge is fallen down !* —

Fallen down ! "

Homeless wanderers such as he,

Fugitive from fortune's frown,

Haply may my playmates be !

IX.

Laughing, rollicking, frolicking Bess
Became an Australian shepherdess ;
For she married a fellow, who one fine day,
Poached, and was sent to Botany Bay.
But to her husband clung our Bess,
In his shame and in his disgrace,
And she helped him to hold up his face,
And get them a home in the wilderness.
There they stumbled on gold, and came
Into America, just before
The breaking out of the civil war,
Whence he emerged with rank and fame,
Stolen cotton and rotten beef
Stamped him murderer and thief!
But the press became his bawd,
And for hire concealed the fraud !
Trump and cannon hailed him chief !

Then with his fame and gold, he won
A place in Congress, at Washington.
There his wife is a star, of course,
Mrs. General Wilberforce!
He? his vote is always sure
For the oppressors of the poor!
When with him our Bessie pleads,
Telling of the poor man's needs,
Telling him of childhood's days, —
To the pleading of her eyes,
In the pauses of her sighs,
The besotted monster says:
" He will vote for London Bridge,
If to place and privilege,
To the fortunate and rich
It devote a special niche:
But the London Bridge they made,
When she with her playmates played,

It is fallen — fallen down !

Fill the cup till memory drown !

He had dropped his childhood off !

Men are but a hoggish host,

In a scramble for the trough,

And the biggest gets the most !"

X.

Lucy went to the hall as maid,

On sped the years, and still she stayed ;

Modest, humble, satisfied,

There she stayed till the lady died,

Stayed and took the keys in her hands,

While the earl withdrew to foreign lands ;

Stayed, and ate of angels food —

The communion of the good ;

For she loving converse held,

With the sages who of eld

Caused our English tongue to rise
To the level of the skies ;
Drank she of the living well,
Pure and inexhaustible,
Of philosophy and song,
Draughts that made her spirit strong,
And that drew her from the plain,
Where, too oft her sex remain,
E'en through grossness dense as night
Delved, as miners delve for coal,
Changing it to glorious light,
In the alembic of her soul !
Soothed by the gentle touch of the years,
The earl found solace for his tears ;
And, 'neath that sky whose folds beneath
His loved one lay, again could breathe ;
And could endure again to tread
Where lay the ashes of his dead.

When he returned, he found the fair,

And ripe, and matronly Lucy there.

Was she beneath him? Not if youth,

And beauty and a soul of truth,

And sterling sense, and manners frank,

May compensate for lack of rank,

Lack of rank? The man who can

Keep through life his soul erect,

True to God and true to man, —

He is peer, of God elect!

For her dower our Lucy brought

Such a soul illumed with thought,

She had left the dregs and lees,

And had culled from learning's page

Honey, pure as that which bees

Cull from California sage.

She brought to him a life untaint;

She brought the virtues of a saint,

If such inhere in living woman,
And be not wholly superhuman.
He brought his wealth and rank, and she
God's patent of nobility !
If there condescension were
It was not from him to her,
Well, they were wed, and she became
Thereby the Lady Lucy Græme !

Lady, lady Lucy Græme !
Though we hold you free from blame,
Yet the feudal heritage
From a past and ruder age,
Park and meadow, glade and lea,
From the mountain to the sea,
Which the barons, stout and fierce,
Won and held with bows and spears, —
Golden leaflet, wreath of pearl,
Which are brought you by the earl, —

These, though you be free from blame,
Though we deem you all the same,
In your leal and noble heart,
Wrest you from your mates apart.
They for bread may toil and sweat,
While your temples you encrown,
With a jeweled coronet!

" *London Bridge is fallen down!* —
Fallen down! — *fallen down!*

           My fair lady! "

XI.

O youth and love! The light and melody
Of life! whereof our souls grow weary ne'er,
Stale, flat, and unprofitable, albeit, be
All else: — and palling on the eye and ear;
Making us look with longing to the bier!

Love came to Lily's youth, a morning star
Of opaline dawn, that ever shone more clear.
Love, as the morning from his radiant car,
Signaled to Hope, upon the luminous heights
    afar.

So wrote our Midge of Lily.   But she sung
Herself a homelier strain, with voice as sweet
As ever starling, in the dews, among
The orange-blooms, or bobolink in the wheat,
Frank, cheerful, kind, unsullied with deceit ;
Full of all human impulse, good and true ;
Sure of her lover, whom she knew complete
In manliness ; into her love she grew!
And carolled oft such song, as here we give
    to you.

Bob, the banker, came to me,
Asking me his wife to be,
He has money, he has lands,
He has soft and dainty hands ;
But my heart it was not free,
And he could not wed with me.
Nay, I shall be, for I can
Be the wife of a workingman.

" Little Lily, go with me,
Mistress of my fate to be ;
Maids are waiting your commands,
And you need not soil your hands."
That was what he said, but I
Curtly gave him this reply :
" Nay, I will be, for I can
Be the wife of a workingman ! "

I know some one I'll confess,
Who he is you cannot guess :
But he is so wise and strong,
And his life so free from wrong !
I'll not wear a satin dress ;
I'll not lounge in idleness ;
But I shall be, for I can,
Be the wife of an honest man !

.   .   .   .

Little Lily ! Alas, alas !
She is lying under the grass !
In the village cold and still,
Among the marbles under the hill !

O she was beautiful that day !
We had crowned her Queen of May ;
Then her cheeks were rosy red ;
Rose, no lily, then they said.

Donald was there, so dear to her !

Such a well-matched pair they were !

Proud was he of his bonnie love,

Proud of the mettled steeds he drove.

Gayly, gayly rode they away,

At the close of the festal day.

On the morrow they would wed : —

Ere the morrow, they were dead !

Close to the brink of the Hermit's Ledge,

Close to the precipice's edge,

Reared the steeds, and before us all,

Plunged they down the mountain wall !

Hark to the cry of wild despair !

'Tis the eldritch scream of the steeds, mid
    air !

Down and down to the gulf beneath,
Into the open jaws of death !

O the woful, woful day !
There our mangled darlings lay ! —
Under the dewy sycamore's drip
Arm in arm and lip to lip !

So we laid them under the grass, —
Her and her Donald ! alas, alas !
In the village under the hill,
Lily pale, and cold and still !

XII.

Jack was a brawny lad of eleven ;
Jessie a little girl of seven ;
Playmates true ; but what else were
She to him, or he to her ?

Nought? but something might have been,

At twenty-one and seventeen.

Then the awkward lad began

To reveal the handsome man ;

Then the beauteous maiden stood

Perfect in her womanhood !

Then must to herself confess

Her surpassing loveliness :

Then would e'en in secret blush,

With her conscious passion's flush.

And were this a tale of love,

Here were told what charms inwove,

Here were told what spells inwrought

Heart and hope, and aim and thought,

Every throb of brain and blood,

Like intergrowing bud and bud,

By the gardeners cunning craft,

In a common stock ingraft.

Like the mists that down the side
Of the mountain slowly glide,
As they to the vale descend
Indistinguishably blend ; —
As the silver and the gold
Which the mountain treasuries hold,
Molten by volcanic heat,
Till like ocean tides they beat,
In a common mass are run,
And indissolubly one, —
So that all the chemist's art
Them can nevermore dispart.
Souls thus graft by cunning love,
From each other ne'er remove ;
Spirits thus that interblend,
Heavenward evermore ascend ;
Lives thus molten into one,
Sever not till life is done.

In a cottage by the sea,
Noiselessly, noiselessly,
As the swans on mountain meres,
Floated by their happy years.
As the billows on the seas,
Waved their barley on the lees.
As the breakers at their feet,
Was the blossom of their wheat;
As the voices of the brine,
Was the lowing of their kine;
Plenty for them, many a gift
Dropped into the hand of thrift.
In the grass, the roses 'mong,
Other flowers in time there sprung;
Fun, at even, sported with
Sylvan boys that were no myth:
Echo laughed amid the swirls
Of the laughter of their girls.

Thus, though not above the poor,

Though they led a life obscure,

Though by fortune uncaressed,

Yet in blessing they were blessed.

As if, on some islet sweet,

Where the morning sits to lave

In the clear and glistening wave

The rosy splendors of her feet,

And the happy sea-gulls press

Her, their mistress, to caress ; —

Drifted on the ocean foam, —

Drifted thither by the chance

Of propitious circumstance,

And thereon had found a home,

In the lake within the ridge

Of the encincturing coral, and

Rested on the shining sand,

Fragments borne from London Bridge.

XIII.

Tom and Tilly.   It were as well
If the story were not to tell,
Theirs through life the hardships were
That befall the laborer.
She, a woman ; he, a man ;
They their wedded life began.
What was all their diligence?
Still it brought no recompense,
Children but increased their cares ;
Squalor and disease were theirs,
Lower still they sank in slime !
Every curse but that of crime —
Curse accumulate on curse —
Weighed them down to worse and worse.
Once, indeed, there seemed to ope
In their sky a gleam of hope ;

Some far relative deceased,
Left to them some small bequest ;
And therewith they sought to fly
From untoward destiny,
To the new world in the west, —
To the islands of the blest.
But not thus the fiend of ill
Did they 'scape : he chased them still,
Kept them from whate'er they wished,
Left them sick, impoverished,
Waifs upon a foreign strand,
Strangers in a stranger land.
Little recked they sweat and moil,
So they had but leave to toil.
Hunger made them only too
Glad of anything to do.
Glad to wear out thews and bones
For their famished little ones,

And to shield them from the gaunt
And ghastly skeleton of want.
Huts and palaces of pride,
Wealth and want were side by side.
Yet will like unto its like.
And there came the Pittsburg strike.
Then the sight of torn up tracks,
Merchandise in flaming stacks,
Plunder, havoc, terror, gloom,
As it were the day of doom!
Pillaged depots ; gusty rains
Of cinders from consuming trains ;
Women with disheveled hair,
And with hungry eyes aglare,
And with lean and bony breasts
Showing through their ragged vests,
Burning, screaming, as they were
Ministers of lucifer ! —

And delirous with delight,
Cursing God and cursing man,
Like the dam of Caliban,
Or the fiends of nether night!
London Bridge was fallen down,
'Twixt the country and the town ;
'Twixt the nation's lowly wards,
And its self-anointed lords ;
'Twixt the brawny sons of toil
And the holders of the soil ;
'Twixt the men of horny fists,
And the gloved monopolists!
Over the fallen ways, alas!
Loves no longer pass and pass ;
But a surging gulf divides
More and more the hostile sides :
Bridgeless! as the gulf betwixt
Hell and highest heaven fixed!

But the law is pitiless, and
Laid on Tom its mailed hand.
Poor, poor Tom ! to prison led !
There upon a felon's bed —
There he died !   A felon's shame
Staining the unsullied name
Of a man, who dared defy
His opressors, and to die ! —
Of a man who nobly fought
To secure the right he sought,
Facing death, as brave men ought!
Poor, poor Tom !   To prison led ! —
Poor, poor Tilly ! — lacking bread.
What for her and her babes was left ?
Death, or beggary, or theft !
So, one morn, at break of day,
On her husband's grave she lay.

"Cause unknown," the record saith !
God knows ! She was starved to death!
Ah ! the sorrows of the poor !
Ah ! the woes they must endure !
Yet a fearful reckoning
Comes for nabob and for king !
If the few will sate their greed,
Reckless of the hosts that need : —
If the laws be framed to hedge
Precedent and privilege,
And the masses are to be
Serfs to a plutocracy, —
God himself will judge the cause,
In defiance of the laws !
What to Him is screed or scrawl ?
He will nullify it all !
In His anger infinite
He will make a mock of it !

By and by the land shall rock,

As there were an earthquake shock !

Then revenge shall lick her lips !

Then at noon shall be eclipse !

And, as when a comet sweeps

Baleful from the upper deeps,

Then the purple air shall hiss

With the scourge of Nemesis !

If the earth your feet beneath,

Ye have sown with dragon's teeth,

Ye shall rue the harvest when

Spring they up as armed men !

XIV.

On the steps was little Midge,

Watching the play of London Bridge ;

In a hazy and dreamy way,

Wondering at the simple play ;

Wondering what would happen when
They were grown to women and men.
Child she was, and to her breast,
Childlike she her dolly pressed ;
Child she was, but not by years
Measure we the lives of seers ;
Little can material cause
Gage the spirit's finer laws ;
Or discern what subtle sense
Antedates experience,
And the gifted child endows
With the poet's ample brows.
Hers the spirit-luminous eye,
Wherefrom speaketh poesy!
Hers such soul as finds a tongue
In the notes of deathless song ;
As if angels touched its keys
To celestial harmonies.

So she watched her mates at play,
In a weird and absent way,
And their destiny forecast
As it were already passed,
Humming in an undertone
" *London Bridge is fallen down !*
Fallen down ! — fallen down !
London Bridge is fallen down !
                    My fair lady ! "
" Some in dusty roads, and brown,
Some in alleys green and shady,
Through the country, through the town,
Hither, thither, they are strown,
Scattered, scattered, far and wide,
As the drift by wind and tide."
While she to her dolly clung,
Thus the little dreamer sung.

Yet the elfin prophetess,

Fairy sibyl, could she guess

What the gifts and graces were

Which the future held for her?

Goodness grew until full-orbed

It into itself absorbed

All her life, and that became

But a self-consuming flame.

Yet, although thereto she brought,

Genius, labor, culture, thought,

In her unassuming eyes

All too small the sacrifice.

Then the curate, when she stood

At the gate of womanhood,

Came and saw, was conquered, and

Wooed and won her, heart and hand.

In his work, henceforth, to his

Dante, she was Beatrice;

To his Numa, fitlier say,

She was the Egeria,

Teaching him to legislate

Wisely for his little State.

So, inspired of her he wrought,

Entering the homes of all,

Lowly hut and lordly hall ;

So, inspired of her, he taught

How our social order is

By opposing force upheld ; —

How, diverse, our interests weld

Battlements and buttresses.

Turbulent our passions roll,

Separating soul from soul ;

But, if all regard the good

Of the human brotherhood,

And respect the rights of each,

As the blessed gospels teach ;

If, with just and equal laws,
We protect the poor man's cause ; —
If, across the muddy tide,
Love and faith, from side to side,
Mutual help and cheer shall flit,
Then, shall struggle stronger knit,
O'er the ever-flowing stream,
Truss to truss, and beam to beam ;
And the arches overspan
All that separates man and man.
But the common bond will break,
If the strong forsake the weak ; —
If your wealth despise your want,
And your wise your ignorant ;
If insatiate as sharks
Be your moneyed oligarchs,
And their hankering for flesh
Daily glut with victims fresh.

While, a wasting skeleton,
Sullen hunger gnaws his bone!
If his moan ye will not hear,
Or give answer with a sneer.
As for Tom, the curate said,
He was foolish and misled.
It was utterest lack of sense
To resort to violence ;
It was useless ; and, beside,
Howsoever justified
The impoverished might be
In resisting tyranny,
Where the few held lordly sway,
And the many must obey! —
In a commonwealth which has
No hereditary class,
And the veriest pauper there
Might become a millionaire, —

In a country where the poll
To the people gives control,
And the fortresses of law
Towers adamantine, draw
Their impenetrable wall
Round the equal rights of all,
Madness was at highest pitch
Whether men were poor or rich,
To resort to force and war,
Whatsoever it was for.
Still, not always could endure,
The forbearance of the poor.
Men were better in their graves,
Than to be but galley slaves!
Yet, upon the wail for food,
There may rise a cry for blood!
When insatiate murder shall,
In your streets hold carnival!

Then shall London Bridge go down,

'Twixt the noble and the clown,

'Twixt the rich in lordly state

And the Lazarus at his gate!

Howsoe'er it come, be sure

There is succor for the poor!

Strong must be the arm that stems

In its wrath the flooded Thames!

Stronger far an arm that may

Stem the floods that vengeful day

Weighted with their shields and spears

Sinks the sovereign with his peers!

Knight and champion, glaived and helmed,

By the waves are overwhelmed!

They that in their chariots ride —

Down they plunge beneath the tide!

So the surging sea shall go

O'er the hosts of Pharaoh!

5

Horse and rider, overthrown,
In the Red sea shall they drown !
But, through seas of blood, shall God
Lead his little ones, dry shod !
By the nymph Egeria taught,
Thus the curate preached and wrought,
Thus he wisely sought to build
London Bridge 'twixt guild and guild !

For Heaven holds men of one degree,
An equal born fraternity.

BOOKS OF BIOGRAPHY.

James A. Garfield. By C. C. Coffin, (War Correspondent "Carleton.") With Portrait. Illustrated. 12mo. $1.50

The Life of General Garfield, written by an author of such brilliant reputation, should be in every library.

" Admirably told." — *Senator Geo. F. Hoar.*

" Exceedingly satisfactory." — *Mrs. General Garfield.*

Charles Jewett, M. D. By William M. Thayer, author of Lives of Lincoln, Washington, Garfield, &c. With Portrait. 12mo. $1.50.

Dr. Jewett's brilliant talents, his wit and humor, and his consecration to the work, have given him the foremost place among Temperance workers at home and abroad.

" Immensely entertaining." — *Rev. T. L. Cuyler, D.D., in New York Evangelist.*

Charles Sumner. By William L. Cornell, LL. D., and Bishop Gilbert Haven, D.D. With the leading Eulogies. With Portrait. Illustrated. 12mo. Cloth. $1.50.

These Eulogies, by the leading men of the nation, are masterpieces of thought and expression, invaluable to every professional man, student, and public speaker.

Phineas Stowe and Bethel Work. Compiled by Rev. H. A. Cooke. 12mo. Cloth, gilt and black. $1.50.

The story of Mr. Stowe's work among the sailors, the intemperate, and the fallen, is full of inspiration, and is as thrilling as a novel.

" Happily adapted to preserve the memory of a singularly useful and noble life, and to stimulate emulation of the rare virtues that shone in the character of Phineas Stowe." — *Daily Advertiser, (Boston.)*

Life, Letters, and Wayside Gleanings. By Mrs. B. H. Crane. Octavo. $2.00.

Mrs. Crane gives not only the history of a family and a life, but she has interwoven recollections of the olden time, incidents and lessons of great interest and value.

" A charming book for the home and fireside."— *Watchman, (Boston.)*

Log-Cabin to White House. By W. M. Thayer, author of " The Bobbin Boy," " Pioneer Boy," &c. 12mo. $1.50.

A Boys' Life of President Garfield. Fascinating and invaluable to boys and young men.

. *Any of these books mailed, postpaid, on receipt of price. Descriptive Catalogue of our Publications free.*

JAMES H. EARLE, Publisher,

20 Hawley Street, Boston, Mass.

BOOKS OF TRAVEL, HEALTH, &c.

The Pictorial Cabinet of Marvels. Comprising History, Science, Discovery, Invention, Natural History, Travel, Art, and Adventure. Illustrated with full-page engravings and plates in colors. Large royal octavo. Elegantly bound in magnificent gilt and black sides. Gilt edges. A superb illustrated Gift Book. $2.50.

Grandmamma's Letters from Japan. By Mrs. Mary Pruyn. Illustrated. 16mo. Cloth, $1.00.

Mrs. Pruyn, one of the leading ladies of Albany in social position and benevolent enterprise, is widely known for her work in Japan. These letters should be in every home and Sunday-school library.

"Mrs. Pruyn is a close and intelligent observer."— *Evening Journal, Albany.*

Sketches of Palestine. A Description of Scenes in the Holy Land and the East, all in verse. By Rev. E. P. Hammond. With steel Portraits of Mr. and Mrs. Hammond, the tour having been their wedding trip. 16mo. Cloth, 75c.

"The main features of the long journey are seen as in panoramic views. The book is full of Jesus and the Gospel. Hundreds who would not read a sermon will gladly read this, though it is full of sermons."— *Christian News.*

Travels in Bible Lands. By Rev. Emerson Andrews. 16mo. 17 illustrations. Cloth, 80c.

Contains letters written by Mr. Andrews during one of his visits to the Lands of the Bible. Talks on religious subjects are interspersed. The work is suited specially to youthful readers.

Tact, Push and Principle. By William M. Thayer. 12mo. 370 pages. Cloth, $1 50.

A book for every young man. Gives the elements, principles, and methods of success. Shows that character and success are not in opposition, and illustrates its points and suggestions from the lives of successful men, showing how they succeeded, and inspiring every young man to make the very most of himself.

The Human Body and Health. By E. Small, M.D. 12mo. 432 pages. Illustrated. $1.50.

A book that should be in every household, and with which old and young should become familiar. It treats of the body and the functions and use of its many parts, the laws of health, &c., and all from the standpoint of a Christian physician.

*** *Any book mailed, postpaid, on receipt of price. Catalogue of our publications free.*

JAMES H. EARLE, Publisher,

20 Hawley St., Boston, Mass.

DEVOTIONAL BOOKS.

Mother Munroe; or, THE SHINING PATH. By Mrs. Mary D. James. Handsome 16mo. With Portrait. 75 cts.

The record of the life of one of the most saintly women of the age.

" Perfect trust and perfect rest seemed the sole tenants of her heart." — *President Wm. F. Warren, D.D.*

Lessons of Trust. By L. B. E., author of " How I Found Jesus." Elegant 16mo. Cloth, 75 cts.; paper, 40 cts.

For all who would serve the Lord with gladness. Abounds in comfort and helpfulness for hours of trouble and temptation.

" From significant initial letters, we suppose the volume is from the pen of the accomplished and devout wife of the publisher. It is a delightful and profitable manual for hours of meditation."—*Zion's Herald,* (*Boston.*)

The Blood of Jesus. By Rev. William Reid, D. D. 18mo. Cloth, 35 cts.

Very clearly and helpfully sets forth, in language that all can understand, the ground of peace with God.

The Gift of God. By Theodore Monod. 16mo. Cloth. 50 cts.

" Simple, clear, and very sweet presentations of Christ, God's unspeakable Gift." — *New York Christian Advocate.*

Calls to Christ. By Rev. W. R. Nicoll, M.A. 16mo. Cloth. 50 cts.

Designed for Christian workers in the awakening of the unconverted.

Little Ones in the Fold. By Rev. E. P. Hammond. 16mo. Cloth. 60 cts.

Contains many instances of conversion of children, and enforces the duty and hopefulness of work to bring them to Jesus early in life.

The Rest of Faith. By Rev. A. B. Earle, D.D. Cloth. 40 cts.

Unfolds the believer's privilege, and shows how the soul may abide in sweet rest, amid all the cares and temptations of life.

** *Any of the above books mailed, postpaid, on receipt of price. Descriptive Catalogue of our Publications free.*

JAMES H. EARLE, Publisher,

20 Hawley Street, Boston, Mass.

BOOKS FOR CHRISTIAN WORKERS

Hand-Book of Revivals. By Rev. H. C. Fish, D.D. 12mo. Cloth. $1.50.

Treats every element of revival work, — indications, hindrances, objections, means, and methods: preaching, prayer, and singing; evangelists, inquirers, converts, Sunday schools, &c.

"There is not in this work, so far as we have been able to discover, any single phase belonging to a genuine revival left unnoticed." — *Christian at Work, (New York.)*

Bringing in Sheaves. By Rev. A. B. Earle, D. D. With Portrait. 12mo. Cloth. $1.50.

This work, drawn from the author's experience, is invaluable to all who would be successful workers for Christ.

"Nothing has for a long time been published, better adapted to arouse holy zeal in the cause of Christ." — *Methodist, (New York.)*

Revivals, and How to Promote Them. By Rev. Orson Parker. 12mo. With Portrait. Cloth. $1.75.

This work is the fruit of the author's experience in revivals for forty years, and is intended to be a practical guide in revival work.

"It is a volume for the hour." — *Zion's Herald.*

Harvest Work of the Holy Spirit, as illustrated in Rev. E. P. Hammond's labors in England, Scotland, and America. 12mo. Cloth. $1.00.

Revival Sermons. By Rev. Emerson Andrews. 12mo. Cloth. With Portrait. $1.25.

This volume contains fifty-four condensed sermons by this revival preacher.

Life, Labors, and Bible Studies of Rev. George F. Pentecost. Edited by P. C. Headley, under Mr. Pentecost's supervision. 12mo. With Portrait. $1.50.

Mr. Pentecost's life has been one of remarkable interest. His Bible readings, for richness and suggestiveness, are, as Joseph Cook says of them, " mountain summits laden with the dew of Hermon."

. Any of the above books mailed, postpaid, on receipt of price. Descriptive Catalogue of our Publications free.

JAMES H. EARLE, Publisher,

20 Hawley Street, Boston, Mass.

www.ingramcontent.com/pod-product-compliance
Lightning Source LLC
Chambersburg PA
CBHW021539270326
41930CB00008B/1310